PALEO INDIAN COOKBOOK
31 Flavorful Quick and Easy Recipes

Disclaimer
Copyright © 2014 by Mary Scott

Disclaimer and Terms of Use: Effort has been made to ensure that the information in this book is accurate and complete, however, the author and the publisher do not warrant the accuracy of the information, text and graphics contained within the book due to the rapidly changing nature of science, research, known and unknown facts and internet. The Author and the publisher do not hold any responsibility for errors, omissions or contrary interpretation of the subject matter herein. This book is presented solely for motivational and informational purposes only.

The recipes and information provided in this report are for educational purposes only and are not intended to provide dietary advice. Readers are strongly encouraged to consult a doctor before making the dietary changes that are required when switching to a Paleo food lifestyle. Recipe directions are provided as a guideline only as the quality of kitchen appliances varies and could result in the need for longer or shorter cooking times. All precautions should be taken to ensure food is fully cooked in order to prevent risk of foodborne illnesses. The author and publisher do not take responsibility for any consequences that are believed to be a result of following the instructions in this book.

Introduction

The word 'Paleo' comes from eating habits of our ancestors. The primal man was fit, strong, healthy and active. Animal's flesh, vegetables, fruits, and nuts were the only things available to eat.

Modern man, due to stress, work and competition, has opted for shortcut meals, which eventually lead to an unhealthy lifestyle. Health conscious people opt for specific diets to stay healthy and fit.

The Paleo Diet is based on the food patterns of primal man. There is a strict list of allowed and forbidden foods that has to be followed. Allowed foods include all the non- vegetarian options like poultry, beef, duck, sea food, pork, lamb; non-starch vegetables, fruits like berries, apple, avocado, plums, watermelon, papaya, mango etc. Nuts and seeds that are allowed include cashew nuts, almonds, macadamia nuts, hazelnuts, pecans, walnuts, pine nuts, pumpkin seeds, melon seeds and sunflower seeds. Of course, there is some quantity of oil also required to cook the food, allowed oils include olive oil, coconut oil, avocado oil, and macadamia oil.

There is a long list of forbidden foods in a Paleo plan. You should totally eliminate dairy products (yes, even milk), grain flours, starch containing foods like potato, rice etc, grains, all beans, lentils, vegetable oils, sweets, aerated drinks, processed sugar, and processed foods.

India is situated at the south margin of Asia. This peninsular country is known for its rich and varied culture, heritage, and food. The diversity of Indian culture is reflected in its food. Every state of India has something unique and special to offer, and surprisingly has got its own cuisine. Combining all, Indian food has much to offer, and only a very small sample is included in this report.

Indian recipes can also be re-formulated as per Paleo guidelines. The unique thing about Indian recipes is that you don't actually feel restricted on a Paleo diet. Delicious and sumptuous recipes can be made with the allowed foods without compromising on taste.

Table of Contents

Breakfast

Spicy Egg Bhurji

Scrambled Eggs with Indian Spices
Serves: 4
Nutritional Information (per serving)

Calories	Carbs	Fat	Protein	Sodium	Sugar
97.0	3.2 g	6.5 g	6.1 g	64 mg	0.8 g

Ingredients
4 Eggs
1 Large Onion, chopped
1 Green or red Fresno peppers, chopped
2 tbsp. Scallion greens, chopped
¼ tsp. Turmeric powder (if available)
½ tsp. Paprika
Sea salt as per taste
2 tsp. Olive oil

Directions
In a non-stick pan, heat oil and sauté the onions for a minute. Add chopped Fresno peppers, scallion greens, turmeric powder, paprika, salt, and sauté well for 2 minutes. Break eggs directly into the pan and agitate. Cover with lid and let it cook on low flame for 5 minutes. Remove the lid and scramble it well. Serve hot.

Paleo Upma

Cauliflower mash with vegetables
Serves: 4
Nutritional Information (per serving)

Calories	Carbs	Fat	Protein	Sodium	Sugar
97.9	14.3 g	3.9 g	4.8 g	74.2 mg	0.8 g

Ingredients

1 Large cauliflower head
¼ cup Carrot, chopped
½ cup Red, yellow and green bell pepper, chopped
1 Medium onion, chopped
½ tsp. Ground black pepper
7-8 Curry leaves (optional)
¼ tsp. Mustard seeds
Sea salt as per taste
1 tbsp. Olive oil

Directions

In a pot, boil water and blanch cauliflower florets for 2 minutes. Drain and cool the florets. Process in a food processor and keep aside.

In a non-stick pan, heat oil and add mustard seeds. When they start to splutter, add curry leaves and chopped onion, and sauté for 30 seconds. Add chopped carrot and bell pepper, sauté for 2 minutes. Add salt, pepper and cauliflower mash; mix well. Cook for another minute. Serve hot.

Paleo Poha

Paleo version of Indian breakfast recipe usually made with rice flakes

Serves: 4

Nutritional Information (per serving)

Calories	Carbs	Fat	Protein	Sodium	Sugar
102.6	15.2 g	4.1 g	5.1 g	68.1 mg	0.6 g

Ingredients
1 Large cauliflower head
1 Medium onion, chopped
1 Large Tomato, chopped
1 Green chili, chopped
7-8 Curry leaves (optional)
¼ tsp. Mustard seeds
¼ tsp. Cumin seeds
¼ tsp. Turmeric powder (if available)
Sea salt as per taste
1 tbsp. Lemon juice
1 tbsp. Olive oil

Directions
Grate cauliflower head to get a rice-like texture. Set aside.
In a non-stick pan, heat oil and add mustard and cumin seeds. When they start to splutter, add curry leaves and chopped onion, and sauté for 30 seconds. Add sea salt, turmeric powder and chopped green chili. Add chopped tomatoes and cook they turn soft. Add grated cauliflower 'rice' and mix well. Cook for a minute and sprinkle lemon juice. Serve hot.

Lunch

Chicken Korma

Spicy and aromatic chicken dish prepared in rich gravy
Serves: 4
Nutritional Information (per serving)

Calories	Carbs	Fat	Protein	Sodium	Sugar
185.7	4.7 g	8.1 g	23.2 g	110.6 mg	0 g

Ingredients
1 lb. Chicken pieces, with bones
1 Large onion, sliced
1 tsp. Ginger-garlic paste
2 Dry red chilies (optional)
2 Medium tomatoes, chopped
¼ tsp. Turmeric powder (if available)
½ tsp. Paprika
½ tsp. Cumin powder
½ tsp. Coriander powder
4 Peppercorns
2 Cloves
1 cinnamon stick, about 2"
1 Bay leaf
Sea salt to taste
Handful of fresh cilantro, chopped
1 tbsp. Olive oil
¼ cup water
Directions
In a non-stick skillet, heat ½ tbsp. oil and add peppercorns, cloves, cinnamon, dry red chilies and bay leaf; sauté for 10 seconds. Add sliced onions and sauté until it starts caramelizing. Take out the caramelized onions and whole spices. Cool down and grind to form a paste.

In the same skillet, heat remaining ½ tbsp. oil and add chicken pieces. Sauté the chicken pieces over high flame for 2 minutes. Reduce the flame and add turmeric powder, paprika, cumin powder, coriander powder, ginger-garlic paste and sauté well for 2 minutes. Add chopped tomatoes and cook until they turn soft. Add onion and spice paste, salt, and water and let it cook on low flame with lid on for 10 minutes.

Remove the lid and add chopped cilantro. Serve hot with cauliflower rice or paleo-friendly bread.

Eggplant Mash

Spicy mashed eggplant recipe with a smoky flavor
Serves: 4
Nutritional Information (per serving)

Calories	Carbs	Fat	Protein	Sodium	Sugar
77.6	10.7 g	3.8 g	2.1 g	8.7 mg	0.1 g

Ingredients
12 oz. Large eggplants
1 Large Onion, chopped
2 Medium tomatoes, chopped
4 Garlic cloves
¼ tsp. Turmeric powder (if available)
½ tsp. Paprika
½ tsp. Cumin powder
Sea salt as per taste
Handful of fresh cilantro, chopped
1 tbsp. Olive oil

Directions
Rub a little oil over eggplant and prick it at few places. Insert garlic cloves in the slits and roast it over low flame until the skin peels out and eggplant becomes soft from deep inside. Cool down and peel out the burnt skin. Mash it in a bowl along with the garlic.

In a non-stick pan, heat oil and sauté the chopped onion until it turns golden. Reduce the flame and add chopped tomatoes and cook until they turn soft. Now, add turmeric powder, paprika, cumin powder, salt, and sauté well for 2 minutes. Add mashed eggplant and let it cook on low flame with lid on for 8-10 minutes.

Add chopped cilantro. Serve hot.

Stir Fried Okra

Spicy Okra recipe with tangy flavor
Serves: 4
Nutritional Information (per serving)

Calories	Carbs	Fat	Protein	Sodium	Sugar
73.7	9.4 g	3.8 g	2.9 g	12.9 mg	2.8 g

Ingredients
1 lb. Okra, cut into 1" pieces
2 Medium tomatoes, chopped
4 Garlic cloves, chopped
¼ tsp. Turmeric powder (if available)
½ tsp. Paprika
½ tsp. Cumin powder
Sea salt as per taste
1 tbsp. Lemon juice
1 tbsp. Olive oil

Directions
In a non-stick pan, heat oil and sauté chopped garlic until it turns golden. Add okra pieces and stir fry for 2 minutes. Also add lemon juice while stir frying, as it will give a bright green color to the dish. Reduce the flame and add turmeric powder, paprika, cumin powder, salt, and sauté well for 2 minutes. Add chopped tomatoes and cook until they turn soft. Serve hot.

Keema Asparagus

Minced lamb with asparagus and spices
Serves: 4
Nutritional Information (per serving)

Calories	Carbs	Fat	Protein	Sodium	Sugar
319.4	9.7 g	21.1 g	23.7 g	14.4 mg	0 g

Ingredients
1 lb. Minced or ground lamb
4 oz. Asparagus, chopped
1 Large Onion, chopped
2 Medium tomatoes, chopped
1 tsp. Ginger-garlic paste
¼ tsp. Turmeric powder (if available)
½ tsp. Paprika
½ tsp. Cumin powder
½ tsp. Coriander powder
Sea salt as per taste
1 tbsp. Olive oil
½ cup Water
Handful of fresh cilantro, chopped
Hot spice powder:
5 Peppercorns
2 Cloves
¼ tsp. Fennel seeds
¼ tsp. Ground nutmeg
1 cinnamon stick, about 2"
1 Bay leaf

Directions
Dry roast the hot spice powder ingredients and cool down. Grind it to form a powder.

In a skillet, heat oil and add minced or ground lamb. Sauté over high flame for 5 minutes until the moisture dries up. Reduce the flame and add chopped onion and ginger-garlic paste; sauté for 2 minutes until the raw smell fades away. Add turmeric powder, paprika, cumin powder, coriander powder, prepared hot spice powder and sauté well for 2 minutes. Add chopped tomatoes and cook until they turn soft. Add water, salt and let it cook on low flame with lid on for 20-25 minutes. Remove the lid and cook more to dry up the moisture, if it is left.

Add chopped cilantro and serve hot.

Broccoli and Bell Pepper Curry

Broccoli and bell peppers in tomato gravy
Serves: 4
Nutritional Information (per serving)

Calories	Carbs	Fat	Protein	Sodium	Sugar
99.7	14.7 g	4.2 g	4.6 g	35.1 mg	1.2 g

Ingredients
1 Large broccoli head, cut into florets
1 Small Red bell pepper, diced
1 Small Green bell pepper, diced
1 Small Yellow bell pepper, diced
4 Tomatoes, diced
1 Large onion, diced
¼ tsp. Turmeric powder (if available)
½ tsp. Paprika
½ tsp. Cumin powder
½ tsp. Coriander powder
Sea salt as per taste
1 tbsp. Dry fenugreek leaves or Cilantro
1 tbsp. Olive oil

Directions
In a processor, put together tomatoes, onions, paprika, turmeric powder, cumin powder, and coriander powder. Process it to make puree.
In a pan, heat 1 tsp. oil and add puree. Sauté it for a minute and then add salt and cook it covered for 10-15 minutes. Keep aside.
In another pan, heat remaining oil and stir fry broccoli florets for 5 minutes. Add bell peppers and sauté for 2 minutes. Now, add the cooked puree and cook for 5 minutes more.
Garnish with dry fenugreek leaves or cilantro. Serve hot.

Shahi Chicken

Mild chicken dish prepared in rich coconut gravy
Serves: 4
Nutritional Information (per serving)

Calories	Carbs	Fat	Protein	Sodium	Sugar
228.4	6.6 g	11.4 g	24.5 g	107.2 mg	2.7 g

Ingredients
1 lb. Chicken pieces, with bones
1 Large Onion, diced
1 tsp. Ginger-garlic paste
4 tbsp. Tomato puree
¼ tsp. Turmeric powder (if available)
½ tsp. Paprika
½ tsp. Cumin powder
½ tsp. Coriander powder
2 tbsp. Cashew nuts, soaked in water
2 tbsp. Coconut milk
Sea salt as per taste
Handful of fresh cilantro, chopped
1 tbsp. Olive oil
¼ cup water

Directions
In a processor, process diced onions and ginger garlic paste to form puree.
In a non-stick pan, heat oil and add onion and ginger-garlic puree; sauté for 5 minutes until raw smell goes away. Add chicken pieces and sauté for 2 minutes. Add turmeric powder, paprika, cumin powder, coriander powder, and sauté well for 2 minutes. Add tomato puree and cook covered for 10-15 minutes.

Grind soaked cashew nuts with some water to form a smooth paste. Add this paste, salt and coconut milk to the chicken and cook for 5 minutes while stirring.
Garnish with chopped cilantro. Serve hot.

Chicken Hariyali

Chicken dish prepared in flavorful green gravy

Serves: 4

Nutritional Information (per serving)

Calories	Carbs	Fat	Protein	Sodium	Sugar
184.5	3.8 g	8.1 g	23.3 g	118.3 mg	0.3 g

Ingredients
1 lb. Chicken pieces, with bones
1 Large Onion, chopped
1 tsp. Ginger-garlic paste
¼ tsp. Turmeric powder (if available)
½ tsp. Coriander powder
1 tbsp. Coconut milk
Sea salt to taste
1 tbsp. Olive oil
2 cups water
For green curry:
2 cups Spinach
½ cup Cilantro
8-10 Mint leaves
½ tsp. Cumin seeds
4 Garlic cloves
1 tbsp. Lemon juice

Directions

In a pot boil 1 cup water and blanch spinach for 5-7 minutes. Drain and cool. In a processor, process blanched spinach and other green curry ingredients to form a puree.

In a non-stick skillet, heat oil and add onion and ginger-garlic paste. Sauté it for 5 minutes until raw smell goes away. Add chicken pieces and sauté for 5 minutes. Add turmeric powder, coriander powder, and sauté well for 2 minutes. Add green puree and cook covered for 15-20 minutes.

Add salt and coconut milk to the chicken and cook more for 5 minutes. Serve hot.

Stir Fried Prawns

Prawns stir fried with blend of Indian spices
Serves: 4
Nutritional Information (per serving)

Calories	Carbs	Fat	Protein	Sodium	Sugar
159.9	2.5 g	5.5 g	23.3 g	168.9 mg	0.2 g

Ingredients
1 lb. Prawns, deveined and shell removed
4 Garlic cloves, minced
¼ tsp. Turmeric powder (if available)
Sea salt to taste
1 tbsp. Olive oil
Spice powder:
4 Dry red chili peppers
½ tsp. Cumin, whole
½ tsp. Coriander, whole
¼ tsp. Fennel seeds
1 tsp. Dry mango powder

Directions
Dry roast the spice powder ingredients (except dry mango powder). Cool down and grind along with dry mango powder to a coarse consistency. Substitute lemon juice if dry mango powder is not available in your region.
In a non-stick pan, heat oil and sauté the minced garlic for 20 seconds. Add prawns and stir fry on high flame for a minute. Add salt, turmeric powder and, spice powder and cook it for 5 minutes. Do not overcook. Serve hot.

Zucchini Masala

Grilled zucchini served with dry spicy gravy called 'masala'
Serves: 4
Nutritional Information (per serving)

Calories	Carbs	Fat	Protein	Sodium	Sugar
71.0	9.4 g	3.7 g	1.8 g	9.7 mg	2.0 g

Ingredients
1 lb. Zucchini, sliced
1 Medium onion, minced
2 Medium tomatoes, minced
4 Garlic cloves, finely chopped
1" Ginger root, finely chopped
¼ tsp. Turmeric powder (if available)
½ tsp. Paprika
½ tsp. Cumin powder
½ tsp. Curry powder
Sea salt as per taste
1 tbsp. Olive oil

Directions
Rub zucchini slices with some salt and turmeric powder. Heat a grill pan and brush it with some oil. Place zucchini slices and cook until it gets tender. Keep aside.
In a non-stick pan, heat oil and sauté chopped garlic and ginger until they turn golden. Add minced onion and sauté until it turns golden. Add minced tomato and cook for 5 minutes. Add turmeric powder, paprika, cumin powder, curry powder, salt, and cook for 5 minutes.
Place grilled zucchini slices in a plate and pour over the gravy. Serve hot.

Beef Steak Salad

Grilled beef steak with flavorful and tangy salad
Serves: 4
Nutritional Information (per serving)

Calories	Carbs	Fat	Protein	Sodium	Sugar
231.5	7.1 g	11.0 g	27.5 g	77.8 mg	1.1 g

Ingredients
1 lb. Beef Loin (lean)
1 Medium red apple, diced
1 Red onion, sliced
2 Medium tomatoes, diced
4 Garlic cloves, crushed
¼ tsp. Turmeric powder (if available)
½ tsp. Curry powder
Sea salt to taste
½ tbsp. Olive oil

For dressing:
2 Red Fresno or chipotle chili peppers
¼ tsp. Cumin powder
A pinch of Rock salt (sea salt may be substituted)
1 tbsp. Fresh cilantro
1 tbsp. Fresh lime juice
2 tsp. Extra virgin olive oil

Directions
Rub steaks with salt, turmeric powder, and curry powder. Heat a non stick pan and add oil. Cook beef until tender and golden brown on both sides. Cut into chunks. Set aside.
Place dressing ingredients in pestle and crush with mortar to a coarse consistency. In a large bowl, add sliced onions, tomatoes, apples, and pour dressing on top. Toss well and serve with beef chunks.

Dinner

Skillet Chicken

Chicken dish cooked in a heavy bottom skillet with whole spices
Serves: 4
Nutritional Information (per serving)

Calories	Carbs	Fat	Protein	Sodium	Sugar
186.7	4.4 g	8.0 g	23.4 g	105.3 mg	2.2 g

Ingredients

1 lb. Chicken pieces, with bones
1 Large Onion, finely chopped
4 tbsp. Tomato puree
1 tsp. Ginger-garlic paste
¼ tsp. Turmeric powder (if available)
½ tsp. Paprika
1 tsp. Curry powder
4 Peppercorns
2 Cloves
1 cinnamon stick, about 2"
1 tsp. Whole coriander
½ tsp. Whole cumin
2 Dry red chilies (optional)
1 Bay leaf
Sea salt as per taste
Handful of fresh cilantro, chopped
1 tbsp. Olive oil
½ cup water

Directions

In a non-stick heavy bottom skillet, heat oil and add peppercorns, cloves, cinnamon, cumin, coriander, dry red chilies and bay leaf; sauté for 10 seconds. Add chopped onions and sauté until it starts caramelizing. Add chicken pieces and sauté over high flame for 2 minutes. Add ginger-garlic paste and sauté again for 2 minutes. Reduce the flame and add turmeric powder, paprika, and sauté well for 5 minutes. Add tomato puree and cook for 5 minutes. Add water and let it cook on low flame with lid on for 8-10 minutes until chicken gets tender.

Remove the lid and add chopped cilantro. Serve hot.

Gobhi Musallam

Grilled whole cauliflower served with mildly spiced gravy.

Serves: 4

Nutritional Information (per serving)

Calories	Carbs	Fat	Protein	Sodium	Sugar
129.8	16.3 g	6.1 g	6.2 g	73.2 mg	3.0 g

Ingredients

1 lb. Large cauliflower head
1 Large Onion, diced
1 tsp. Ginger-garlic paste
4 tbsp. Tomato puree
¼ tsp. Turmeric powder (if available)
½ tsp. Paprika
½ tsp. Cumin powder
½ tsp. Coriander powder
2 tbsp. Poppy seeds, soaked in warm water
2 tbsp. Coconut milk
Sea salt to taste
Handful of fresh cilantro, chopped
1 tbsp. Olive oil
¼ cup water

Directions

Preheat the oven to 400°F. Wash the cauliflower head thoroughly and pat dry. Rub with salt, paprika and turmeric powder. Brush lightly with cooking spray and grill or bake it at 400°F for 10-15 minutes or until it turns golden and tender.

In a food processor, process diced onions and ginger garlic paste to form puree.

In a non-stick pan, heat oil and add onion and ginger-garlic puree; sauté for 5 minutes until raw smell goes away. Add turmeric powder, paprika, cumin powder, coriander powder, and sauté well for 2 minutes. Add tomato puree and cook covered for 10-15 minutes.

Grind soaked poppy seeds with some water to form a smooth paste. Add this paste, salt and coconut milk to the gravy and cook for 5 minutes while stirring.

Place grilled cauliflower in a plate and pour over the gravy. Garnish with chopped cilantro and serve hot.

Nihari

Beef dish slow-cooked in Crockpot with Indian spices
Serves: 4
Nutritional Information (per serving)

Calories	Carbs	Fat	Protein	Sodium	Sugar
443.5	11.4 g	28.7 g	34.9 g	94.1 mg	1.2 g

Ingredients
1 lb. Beef chuck pot roast, with bones
1 Large Onion, finely sliced
2 Large tomatoes, diced
2 Green chilies, whole
1 tsp. Ginger-garlic paste
¼ tsp. Turmeric powder (if available)
½ tsp. Paprika
1 tsp. Coriander powder
5 Peppercorns
1 cinnamon stick, about 2"
¼ tsp. Ground nutmeg
1 Bay leaf
Sea salt as per taste
1 tbsp. Walnut kernels, chopped
2 tbsp. Coconut flour
1 tbsp. Lemon juice
1 tbsp. Olive oil
1 cup water

Directions
In a pan, heat oil and add beef pieces; sauté on high flame for 2 minutes.
Transfer the beef to a Crockpot and add remaining ingredients. Cook on low heat for 8-10 hours. Serve hot.

Mushroom Spinach Curry

Mushroom recipe prepared in spinach gravy
Serves: 4
Nutritional Information (per serving)

Calories	Carbs	Fat	Protein	Sodium	Sugar
73.0	11.2 g	3.6 g	5.4 g	14.0 mg	1.2 g

Ingredients
1 lb. White button mushroom, thickly sliced
2 cups Spinach
2-3 Green chilies
1 Medium Onion, minced
1 tsp. Ginger, grated
1 tsp. Garlic, finely chopped
¼ tsp. Turmeric powder (if available)
½ tsp. Coriander powder
1 tbsp. Coconut milk
Sea salt as per taste
1 tbsp. Olive oil
2 cups water

Directions
In a pot boil 1 cup water and blanch spinach for 5-7 minutes. Drain and cool. In a processor, process blanched spinach and green chilies to form a puree.
In a non-stick pan, heat oil and sauté the chopped garlic for few seconds. Add onion and grated ginger and sauté it for 5 minutes. Add turmeric powder, coriander powder, and sauté well for 2 minutes.
Add spinach puree and cook covered for 10 minutes. Add mushroom, salt and, coconut milk and cook more for 5 minutes. Serve hot.

Roghan Josh

Exotic lamb recipe prepared with almonds and spices

Serves: 4

Nutritional Information (per serving)

Calories	Carbs	Fat	Protein	Sodium	Sugar
254	10.6 g	12.6 g	25.9 g	95.8 mg	0.5 g

Ingredients
1 lb. Lamb pieces, with bones
1 Large Onion, finely sliced
1 tsp. Ginger-garlic paste
1 tbsp. Grated raw papaya or meat tenderizer
16 Almonds
Sea salt as per taste
Handful of fresh cilantro, chopped
1 tbsp. Olive oil
1½ cup water

Gravy:
3 Large tomatoes, diced
¼ tsp. Turmeric powder (if available)
½ tsp. Paprika
¼ tsp. Cinnamon powder
1 tsp. Curry powder
4 Peppercorns
2 Cloves
1 tsp. Whole coriander
½ tsp. Whole cumin
2 Dry red chilies (optional)
1 Bay leaf

Directions

In a non-stick skillet, heat ½ tbsp. oil and add sliced onions. Sauté until it starts caramelizing. Remove the caramelized onions and cool down.

In a pot, boil water and add all the gravy ingredients. Boil it covered for 10 minutes. Drain and cool, and reserve the water. Transfer the boiled ingredients to a processor, add caramelized onions, almonds and process it to form a puree.

In the same skillet in which onions were caramelized, heat ½ tbsp. oil and add lamb pieces. Sauté over high flame for 5 minutes or until the lamb turns golden brown. Add ginger-garlic paste and sauté again for 5 minutes. Reduce the flame and add the prepared puree and grated raw papaya or meat tenderizer. Cook for 5 minutes. Add the reserved water and let it cook on low flame with lid on for 20-25 minutes until lamb gets tender.

Remove the lid and add chopped cilantro. Serve hot.

Chicken Biryani

Chicken dish cooked with cauliflower 'rice'
Serves: 4
Nutritional Information (per serving)

Calories	Carbs	Fat	Protein	Sodium	Sugar
225.8	14.9 g	5.3 g	31 g	148.9 mg	0 g

Ingredients
1 lb. Boneless chicken breast, cut into 1" cubes
1 Large cauliflower head
1 Medium onion, finely chopped
2 Tomatoes, chopped
1 tsp. Ginger-garlic paste
¼ tsp. Turmeric powder (if available)
½ tsp. Paprika
½ tsp. Coriander powder
½ tsp. All spice powder
1 Bay leaf
Sea salt as per taste
Handful of fresh cilantro, chopped
10-12 Fresh mint leaves
1 tbsp. Olive oil

Directions
In a large bowl, add chicken pieces and all the ingredients (except cauliflower). Mix well and marinate for an hour.
Wash the cauliflower head and pat dry. Grate it to make cauliflower 'rice'.
In a non-stick heavy bottom skillet, add the marinated chicken and all the ingredients. Sauté it over high flame for 5 minutes. Cover and let it cook on low flame with lid on for 10-15 minutes or until chicken gets tender. Cook more to evaporate the moisture. Consistency should be dry.
Add the grated cauliflower and mix well. Cook for 2 minutes. Serve hot.

Kofta Curry

Lamb or Beef meat balls in spicy gravy
Serves: 4
Nutritional Information (per serving)

Calories	Carbs	Fat	Protein	Sodium	Sugar
222.9	7.3 g	12.6 g	26.6 g	16.9 mg	2.3 g

Ingredients
Kofta or meat balls:
1 lb. Minced or ground lamb/beef
2 tbsp. Scallions, finely chopped
5-6 Mint leaves, minced
½ tsp. Ginger root, grated
2 tbsp. Coconut flour
½ Egg, for binding
¼ tsp. Paprika
Sea salt as per taste
Gravy:
1 Large Onion, chopped
4 tbsp. Tomato puree
1 tsp. Ginger-garlic paste
¼ tsp. Turmeric powder (if available)
½ tsp. Paprika
½ tsp. Curry powder
¼ tsp. Cinnamon powder
¼ tsp. Ground nutmeg
Sea salt to taste
1 tbsp. Olive oil
½ cup Water
Handful of fresh cilantro, chopped

Directions

Preheat the oven to 400°F. In a large bowl, add kofta or meat ball ingredients (except egg) and mix well. Beat an egg and add slowly while binding. Add only about ½ egg or less for binding. Make small balls out of the mixture and bake it at 400°F for 20 minutes.

In a wok, heat oil and add chopped onion and ginger-garlic paste; sauté for 2 minutes until the raw smell fades away. Add turmeric powder, paprika, curry powder, cinnamon powder, nutmeg powder, sauté well for 2 minutes. Add tomato puree and cook for 5 minutes. Add water, salt and let it cook on low flame with lid on for 5 minutes. Add baked meat balls and cook for 10 minutes covered with lid.

Add chopped cilantro and serve hot. Serve ideally with zucchini spaghetti.

Navratna Korma

Exotic mixed vegetable recipe prepared in cashew and coconut curry

Serves: 4

Nutritional Information (per serving)

Calories	Carbs	Fat	Protein	Sodium	Sugar
187	20.7 g	10.9 g	4.7 g	24.7 mg	8 g

Ingredients
1 Small broccoli head, cut into florets and blanched
¼ cup Carrot, diced
1 Small Red bell pepper, chopped
1 Small Green bell pepper, chopped
1 Small Yellow bell pepper, chopped
¼ cup Fresh pineapple, diced
½ cup Button mushrooms, diced
2 Green chilies, sliced
1 Large yellow onion, diced
4 Garlic cloves
1 Ginger root, about 2"
½ tsp. White pepper powder
½ tsp. Cumin powder
½ cup Coconut milk
12-14 Cashew nuts, soaked in water
Sea salt as per taste
1 tbsp. Cilantro, chopped
1 tbsp. Olive oil
½ cup Water

Directions

In a pot, boil water and add onion, ginger and garlic. Boil for 5-7 minutes. Cool and drain. Transfer it to a processor and process it to make puree.

In a pan, heat 1 tsp. oil and add puree. Sauté it for 2 minute and then add salt, white pepper powder, cumin powder, coconut milk, and cook it covered for 10 minutes.

Grind soaked cashews to a form a paste and add it to the gravy. Cook for 5 minutes,

In another pan, heat remaining oil and stir fry all the veggies and mushroom for 5 minutes. Now, add the cooked gravy to it and cook for 5 minutes more.

Garnish with cilantro and serve hot.

Fish Curry

Fish cooked in aromatic, spicy and delicious gravy
Serves: 4
Nutritional Information (per serving)

Calories	Carbs	Fat	Protein	Sodium	Sugar
202.2	9.6 g	7.9 g	23 g	99.1 mg	2.4 g

Ingredients
1 lb. fillet of sole, cut into 4 pieces (4 oz. each)
1 Medium Onion, chopped
Sea salt as per taste
Handful of fresh cilantro, chopped
1 tbsp. Olive oil
¼ cup Water
Curry paste:
1 Medium tomato, diced
6 Dry red chili peppers or chipotle chili
½ tsp. Turmeric powder
½ tsp. Whole cumin seeds
1 tsp. Whole coriander seeds
5 Black peppercorns
A Pinch of Fenugreek Seeds (if available)
1 Ginger root, about 2"
3 Garlic cloves
½ cup Coconut, grated
1 tbsp. Tamarind paste

Directions
Blend the curry ingredients in a food processor to form a puree.
In a non-stick pan, heat oil and add onion; sauté for 5 minutes until raw smell goes away. Add puree and sauté for 5 minutes. Reduce the flame and cook covered for 15 minutes.
Add fish fillet, salt, water and cook covered for 10 minutes. Garnish with chopped cilantro. Serve hot.

Butternut Squash Varuval

South Indian Butternut squash dish cooked with delectable flavors

Serves: 4

Nutritional Information (per serving)

Calories	Carbs	Fat	Protein	Sodium	Sugar
128.9	13.2 g	8.7 g	1.7 g	5.1 mg	0.5 g

Ingredients

1 lb. Butternut squash, peeled and cut into 1" cubes
¼ tsp. Mustard seeds
¼ tsp. Turmeric powder (if available)
½ tsp. Paprika
½ tsp. Cumin powder
1 tsp. Mango powder
5-6 Curry leaves or basil
8-10 Roasted pecans
Sea salt as per taste
1 tbsp. Olive oil

Directions

In a non-stick pan, heat oil and add mustard seeds. When it starts spluttering, add curry or basil leaves and immediately add squash cubes. Stir fry for 2 minutes on high flame. Reduce the flame and add turmeric powder, paprika, cumin powder, mango powder salt, and sauté well for 5 minutes. Mix in roasted pecans and serve hot.

Snacks/Starters

Chicken Tikka

Boneless chicken cubes marinated with spices and baked
Serves: 4
Nutritional Information (per serving)

Calories	Carbs	Fat	Protein	Sodium	Sugar
126.1	4.3 g	1.9 g	18.6 g	66 mg	0.5 g

Ingredients
12 oz. Chicken breast fillet, cut into 2" cubes
3 Shallots, halved and layers separated
1 Tomato, diced and deseeded
1 Green bell pepper, diced
1 tsp. Ginger-garlic paste
¼ tsp. Turmeric powder (if available)
½ tsp. Paprika
½ tsp. Coriander powder
½ tsp. All spice powder
Sea salt as per taste
½ tbsp. Lemon juice
½ tbsp. Olive oil

Directions
In a bowl, add all the ingredients and mix well. Add chicken pieces and mix well with the marinated. Marinate it for 4-5 hours in refrigerator. Place the chicken cubes in skewers, alternating with onion layers, tomato and bell pepper dices. Bake it in a preheated oven a 400°F for 20 minutes. Serve hot.

Kakori Kebob

Minced lamb kebobs with aromatic flavors

Serves: 4

Nutritional Information (per serving)

Calories	Carbs	Fat	Protein	Sodium	Sugar
171.6	4 g	11.2 g	19.1 g	9.1 mg	1.5 g

Ingredients
12 oz. Minced lamb meat
1 Medium onion, minced and water squeezed
½ tbsp. Grated raw papaya or meat tenderizer
1 tsp. Ginger-garlic paste
¼ tsp. Turmeric powder (if available)
½ tsp. Paprika
½ tsp. Coriander powder
½ tsp. All spice powder
2 tbsp. Almond flour
1 tbsp. Dry rose petals, crushed
Sea salt as per taste
1 tbsp. Olive oil

Directions
In a bowl, add all the ingredients and mix well (except oil). Place for 3-4 hours in refrigerator. Place the small portions on skewers and flatten it along the length of skewer to give shape of kebob. Brush kebobs with olive oil and bake in a preheated oven at 400°F for 30 minutes. Serve hot.

Muddur Vada

An all-time favorite Indian snack with Paleo twist
Serves: 4
Nutritional Information (per serving)

Calories	Carbs	Fat	Protein	Sodium	Sugar
78.3	7.8 g	5.2 g	1.4 g	3.5 mg	1.4 g

Ingredients
½ cup Acorn squash, grated
½ cup Cabbage, grated
1 Medium onion, thinly sliced
¼ tsp. Turmeric powder (if available)
½ tsp. Paprika
½ tsp. All spice powder
2 tbsp. Almond flour
5-6 Curry leaves or basil, finely chopped
Sea salt as per taste
1 tbsp. Olive oil

Directions
In a bowl, add all the ingredients (except oil) and mix well. Place the mixture in refrigerator for 30 minutes. Make small patties out of the mixture.
Heat oil in a pan and cook the patties on both sides until golden brown. Serve with any dip of your choice.

Crisp Aubergine (Eggplant) Slices

Spicy eggplant slices baked to a crispy texture
Serves: 4
Nutritional Information (per serving)

Calories	Carbs	Fat	Protein	Sodium	Sugar
16.3	3 g	0.1 g	0.7 g	0.1 mg	0 g

Ingredients
8 oz. Aubergines (Eggplants), sliced
¼ tsp. Turmeric powder (if available)
½ tsp. Paprika
½ tsp. Five spice powder
½ tsp. Dry mango powder
Sea salt as per taste

Directions
In a bowl, add all the ingredients (except oil) and mix well. Add aubergine slices and rub the spices on it. Place spiced aubergine slices on a baking sheet and spray it lightly with cooking spray. Bake it in a preheated oven at 400°F for 20 minutes. Serve hot.

Coastal Grilled Fish

Grilled fish with unique flavors from Coastal Indian region
Serves: 4
Nutritional Information (per serving)

Calories	Carbs	Fat	Protein	Sodium	Sugar
178.6	1.2 g	8.9 g	22.5 g	73.2 mg	0.3 g

Ingredients
12 oz. Salmon fillet
¼ tsp. Turmeric powder (if available)
½ tsp. Chili flakes
¼ tsp. Nutmeg powder
¼ tsp. Curry powder
2 tbsp. Almond flour
Sea salt as per taste
1 tbsp. Lemon juice
1 tbsp. Olive oil

Directions
Make superficial slits on fish fillets and apply lemon juice and salt over it. Keep it aside for 5 minutes.
In a bowl, add all the dry ingredients and mix well. Rub the spice mixture over fish fillets well.
Heat oil in a grill pan and cook the fish fillets on both sides until golden and flaky. Serve hot.

Soups

Murg Shorba

Chicken soup with delectable Indian flavors
Serves: 4
Nutritional Information (per serving)

Calories	Carbs	Fat	Protein	Sodium	Sugar
103.1	5.8 g	1.9 g	12.4 g	42.8 mg	2.5 g

Ingredients
8 oz. Boneless chicken, cut into strips
1 Large Onion, finely chopped
½ tsp. Ginger-garlic paste
½ tsp. White pepper powder
2 Fresh red or green chilies, chopped finely
½ tsp. Cumin powder
½ tsp. Cinnamon powder
2 tbsp. Coconut milk
Sea salt as per taste
Handful of fresh cilantro, chopped
1 tbsp. Fresh lime juice
½ tbsp. Olive oil
1½ cups water

Directions
In a non-stick saucepan, heat oil and add chicken strips. Add ginger-garlic paste and sauté for 2 minutes. Take it out, cool down and shred it.
In the same saucepan, add water, salt, white pepper powder, nutmeg powder, and cinnamon powder and bring it to a boil.
Add shredded chicken and cook it on a low flame for 5 minutes. Add coconut milk and cook for 5 minutes more while stirring. Add fresh lime juice and mix well.
Serve hot with freshly chopped coriander.

Green Soup

Healthy green soup with spinach, green tomatoes and cucumber

Serves: 4

Nutritional Information (per serving)

Calories	Carbs	Fat	Protein	Sodium	Sugar
47.3	7.3 g	1.9 g	1.6 g	19.3 mg	3.8 g

Ingredients
3 Green tomatoes
½ Small cucumber, diced
½ cup Spinach
2 tbsp. Celery, chopped
1 tbsp. Lemon grass, minced
4 Garlic cloves, finely chopped
½ tsp. Black pepper powder
½ tsp. Cumin powder
Sea salt as per taste
1 tbsp. Fresh lemon juice
½ tbsp. Olive oil
1½ cups water

Directions
In a pot, boil water with some salt and blanch Green tomatoes. Take out the tomatoes and in same water, blanch the spinach. Drain and cool, reserve the water. In a processor, process together blanched tomatoes, spinach, and cucumber to form a puree.

In a non-stick saucepan, heat oil and sauté chopped garlic for few seconds. Add the puree and cook it for 5 minutes.

Add reserved water, salt, black pepper powder, cumin powder, celery, and lemon grass and bring it to a boil. Add fresh lemon juice and mix well. Serve hot.

Yakhni

Lamb soup with whole spices
Serves: 4
Nutritional Information (per serving)

Calories	Carbs	Fat	Protein	Sodium	Sugar
156.3	6.9 g	5.9 g	18.4 g	57.6 mg	2.5 g

Ingredients
12 oz. Lamb chops
1 Medium Onion, finely chopped
1 tsp. Ginger, grated
5-6 Garlic cloves, crushed
½ tsp. Black pepper powder
2 Fresh green chilies, chopped finely
1 Cinnamon stick, about 2"
4 Peppercorns
2 Cloves
¼ tsp. Nutmeg powder
¼ tsp. Coriander powder
1 Bay leaf
Sea salt as per taste
2 tbsp. Fresh lemon juice
Handful of fresh cilantro, chopped
½ tbsp. Olive oil
1½ cups water

Directions

In a pressure cooker, put lamb pieces and turn on the gas. Sauté it until the moisture dries up.

Add water, salt, peppercorns, cloves, cinnamon, bay leaf, green chilies, ginger, garlic, black pepper powder, nutmeg powder, and coriander powder and bring it to a boil.

Cook under pressure for 15 minutes or till 3 whistles. Open the lid and add lemon juice. Serve hot with freshly chopped coriander.

If you do not have a pressure cooker, cook covered for at least 40-50 minutes on the stove.

This is the 6 x 9 Basic Template. Paste your manuscript into this template or simply start typing. Delete this text prior to use.

CPSIA information can be obtained
at www.ICGtesting.com
Printed in the USA
LVIC04n2226010714
392630LV00002B/7